Praise For

SCREW THE WALL!

In *Screw the Wall*, Juan Manuel Pérez answers the question: what can brown poetry do for you? He does so as he digs in and swings for and at the fences. This book of impactful poetry deals mainly with barriers—barriers erected by poverty, prejudice, culture, and language; barriers imagined and real; barriers conquered, and barriers left to be scaled. These poems range from the humorous, to the satiric, to the poignant, to the nostalgic. A few of these worthwhile works might strike a nerve or two with their readers, but as Pérez reminds us about the border wall in his poem *A Promising Letter to a Worrisome Trump*, "No need to worry; We'll get over it!" Likewise, In *Screw the Wall* Juan Manuel Pérez has hit a home run deep over the wall.

Alan Berecka
author of *The Hamlet of Stittville*
2017-2018 Corpus Christi Poet Laureate

If you have never heard the poetry of Juan Manuel Pérez then you are in for a treat. You must hear his words, as reading them is not enough. He writes the poems that many are afraid to discuss. He writes the poems many will hide from. He writes the poems that all need to hear. His words are diverse and full of compassion, but he speaks the hard truths our Nation struggles with daily. These truths have divided families, increased the struggles for minorities (which are becoming the majority), and left those affected silent and waiting for a chance. Pérez offers words full of insight and empathy and his influences are strong.

Malia A. Pérez, Ed.D.
author of *Everything Depends Upon The Little Things*
2009-2015 World Book Night Ambassador and Three-Time Teacher Of The Year

In his most recent poetry collection, *Screw The Wall! And Other Brown People Poem*s, Juan Manuel Pérez invites us into his soul, beckoning: "I invite you into my soul / Somewhere between Texas and Mexico." And it is in this "somewhere" where his poetry happens: poetry of lived experience, poetry of place, poetry where "America is the land of the lost" and the only thing that will shine a light in its dark path is love. This collection is full of "strong, bronze Chicano poems," and I am reading.

Octavio Quintanilla
author of *Wasted Time*
2018-2020 San Antonio Poet Laureate

SCREW THE WALL
AND OTHER BROWN PEOPLE POEMS

JUAN MANUEL PÉREZ

FlowerSong Press
McAllen, Texas 78501
Copyright © 2020 by Juan Manuel Pérez

ISBN: 978-1-7345617-4-6

Published by FlowerSong Press
in the United States of America.
www.flowersongpress.com

Set in Adobe Garamond Pro

Cover painting by Jose Angel Lozano, oil on canvas "Golden Dream"
www.lazonofineart.com
Typeset and design by Matthew Revert
www.matthewrevert.com
Author photograph by Marah M. Perez, M. Ed.

No part of this book may be reproduced without written permission from the publisher.

All inquiries and permission requests should be addressed to the Publisher.

<u>on "rebellion"</u>
"I hold that a little rebellion now and then is a good thing, and as necessary in the political world as storms in the physical."

Thomas Jefferson
January 1787

<u>on "racism"</u>
"Those who do nothing are inviting shame as well as violence. Those who act boldly are recognizing right as well as reality."

John F. Kennedy
June 1963

<u>on "walls"</u>
"Is there a brick wall getting in your way? Fine. That happens. But you have a choice. You can walk away from the wall. You can go over the wall. You can go under the wall. You can go around the wall. You can also obliterate the wall. In other words, don't let anything get in your way. Get a balance, and then let the positive outdistance the negative."

Donald J. Trump
December 2015

<u>on "a red t-shirt"</u>
"MAGA: MEXICANS ALWAYS GET ACROSS"

lots of t-shirt companies
June 2019

TABLE OF CONTENTS

11	Free
12	Chupacabra Lives Matter
13	It's Not Easy Being Greasy
14	The Onion Picker's Dream
15	Push Farther My Father Said
17	I Am Juan In The Fields
19	Mexicans Appear Violent
21	The Cat From The Other Side Of The Tracks
22	Today We March
24	Mexicans On The Move Again
25	Mexi-Scam
27	The Cure
28	The Trouble With Poets
30	Casual Mexican
31	When Mexicans Attack!
32	Latter Day Mexican Americans
34	Sweet Jesus
36	At The Border Of Ignorance
38	The Plight
39	Are You Tired Of US Yet?
40	What Does It Matter
42	Shallow Water
44	Antebellum Again
45	Gunfighters At Bland Canyon
46	Stereotypical: A Zombie Poem… Or Is It?
47	What To Expect When You're Suspecting
48	Lengua-Legal
49	Those Doors
50	I See Brown People
52	Color
53	What If It Happen In America?
54	For The Mother Of My Half-Mexican Children

55	If I Was White I Would Write…
56	El Corrido De El Librotraficante
58	Prayer Sayer
61	English As A Second Language (ESL) Civics Lesson 1: A Slice Of "The Declaration Of Independence"
64	Holy Sonnet No. 1
65	I Am Chupacabra
67	Jalapeño Propagandist
68	What Can Brown Do For You?
70	Dr. Jesus' Presents: It's "Kiss A Mexican" Everyday
72	Make Tortillas Not War
73	Life Around The Tortilla Curtain
75	Don't Drop The Taco
77	Tell Me What?
78	A Promising Letter To A Worrisome Trump
79	Bad Hombre
81	Humpity Trumpity
83	Screw The Wall!
85	Screw The White Man!
87	Acknowledgements
93	Biography

```
        S
        C
        R
        E
        W
SCREW THE WALL!
        W
        A
        L
        L
        !
```

Free

America, of thee I dream
Land of my fathers
Land of immigrant forefathers
Land of the me
Land of immigrant dreams
America, do you cry for me
For what has been done to me
For what we have done to us
Brown people
Black people
Red people
All people
America, land of the free
Land of the loving
Land of the lost
And looking for a way out of this mess
America, I weep for thee
If this tis of thee
Dare not come again
This Plato's Republic dream
America, this America
I dream of thee
Forever free
American me

Chupacabra Lives Matter

When I say, "Chupacabra Lives Matter"
I mean that imagination matters
I mean that creativity matters
I mean that our freedom to write, matters
I mean that artistic free-will, matters
I mean that everything we do, matters

When I say, "Chupacabra Lives Matter"
I mean that immigrant lives matter too
I mean that symbolism matters
I mean that diversity matters
I mean that being humble matters
I mean that humanity matters too

When I say, "Chupacabra Lives Matter"
I mean that everything God made matters

It's Not Easy Being Greasy

"It's not easy being greasy"
I could hear my father say
But did they call you "Mexican Grease"
Because of what you ate that day

"It's not easy being greasy"
I could hear my father say
But did they call you "Mexican Grease"
Because of what is on your hair today

"It's not easy being greasy"
I could hear my father say
But did they call you "Mexican Grease"
Because you work on cars all day

"It's not easy being greasy"
I could hear my father say
But did they call you "Mexican Grease"
Because in onion fields you sweat and pray

"It's not easy being greasy"
I could hear my father say
But did they call you "Mexican Grease"
Because bigots had no other words to say

The Onion Picker's Dream

Distance
Between me, my father
Sacks of onions, fields of sweat
American born, speaking no English
Yet, well providing for the English-speaking world
Of hand-picked onions for happy, American grills

Distance
Between me, my future
Stacks of books, proliferation of papers
Mexican tested, getting on by
With English picked up from comic books
Where "Batman" was the first English word spoken

Distance
Between me, my ethnicity
Those hot, onion fields so long, long ago
For American classrooms that never, never end
For those that ended many decades ago
Abruptly for my onion-picking father

Distance
Between that boy, this man
Is what I have made of it
Is what I have left to speak for
On improving that long, distance dream
That was originally my father's very own

Push Farther My Father Said

Under a clear, Texas sky
The rain of poverty hit hard
Sacks of onions upon my back
A memory distant, yet not far away

Push farther my father said

This land will be re-conquered, regrown
Season upon season upon season
Like life since, when, then
With onions, onions, and more onions

Push farther my father said

Beyond these fields into others
Where I would not be on my knees
Where the loose dirt would be under me
Not on me, not over me

Push farther my father said

In the only language he knew
That's why I learned this one
To wield the words that would free me
From a lifetime of onion fields

Push farther my father said

I Am Juan In The Fields

I am Juan
I have been born to privilege
Working many migrant fields
With my poorly educated parents
Who allowed me to complete mine

I am Juan
My belly is full
Of beans and tortillas
Fresh, early in the summer morning
In the sea of undocumented brown people

I am Juan
My ears are rich
With the sounds of grunts and groans
Of the onion cutting scissors
Bleeding sweet its sour juices

I am Juan
My body constantly cool
With my precious, Mexican sweat
Taking a break to talk to the onions
Telling them to make a great feast of themselves

I am Juan
I am Juan of the free
I am Juan of the educated

I am Juan of the privilege
I am Juan in the onion fields

Mexicans Appear Violent

One can't be for certain
Yet history does reveal some truth
That no matter how nice they act
Mexicans appear violent

Is it because they lost their great cities
To European conquistadors?
Is it because they were forced
Into a religion that made them awkward?

Is it because after reclaiming their land
The Anglo-Americans came to take half of it?
Is it because after the Americans did that
They also made promises they never intended to keep?

Like the promises they made
With the Mexican's red cousins?
Is it because the Alamo never likes
To claim the Mexicans on her side?

Is it because Mexicans are feared foreign
Dirty vagrants in any culture?
Is it because more than enough of them
Are incarcerated or wrongly accused?

Or is it because others don't know any better?
Or undermine the history of brown culture?

Of course, one can't be sure
As to why they appear so violent

Yet throw them beer and chicharones
To keep them busy and plum fat happy
Then somehow, in some fantastical way
Appearances might be the least of your worries

The Cat From The Other Side Of The Tracks

Do you know that cat
That cat from the other side of the tracks
Where los vatos are all down
In all kinds of shades of brown
Where poverty is spread a good mile wide
Like smooth tortillas all around

So, you know that cat
Can't put it any clearer than that
Handcuffed and taken downtown
Chicano the verb, not the noun
Because colors speak louder than words
Where lineups make minorities frown

Hell, everyone knows that cat
That cat from the west side of the tracks
Where the madrecitas are all trying to make you fat
With menudo and tamales and that
That cat works every low-paying job around town
Can't really miss him unless you're wacked

That semi-illusive cat
That cat from the other side of the tracks
Where speaking Mexican is a real fact
And the good life is all that's that
And the sun sun-shines, yes it shines
On all those cats from the other side of the tracks

Today We March

Today we march
Because César Chávez marched
For farm labor rights in California
For Mexican American civil rights in America
For human rights in the entire world

Today we march
Because Dolores Huerta marched
Showing that Mexican Americans together
Could do more for the field worker, the orchard worker
The un-rich, the lower classes, the real people

Today we march
Because there are those still working those fields, those orchards
Like my family and I did when I was younger
So that there may be fresh vegetables and fruits on your tables
Your stove tops, your party trays, your grills, your drinks

Today we march
Because there are those still working those fields, those orchards
In Tejas, California, Colorado
Anywhere there is a field or an orchard and a job that Americans claim
Is taken by immigrants or their descendants, yet no American really wants

Today we March
Because César Chávez & Dolores Huerta did
Because all those fighting for farm labor rights did
Because all those fighting for Mexican Americans rights did
Because all those fighting for minorities' civil rights did

Today we march
Because we can
Because we need to
Because if we don't, then we're back to where we started
Forgetting that long road that was already paved for us

So, today we march because we can
Si Se Puede! Si Se Puede! Si Se Puede!

Mexicans On The Move Again

The Mexicans are moving to Mars!

What?

Yeah, the Mexicans are moving to Mars.
They figured at least this planet
offered a clean slate
an abundance of land without fences
a kingdom for the new Aztlán

   without gringos to tell them what to clean
   without black guys stealing their women
   without Asians competing for restaurants
   without red cousins to wrestle for government help
   without store clerks with funny accents eyeing them suspiciously
   without Europeans bent on re-conquest
   without fellow brown sellouts snitching too soon to the authorities
   about their goal to run a Chicano in the next presidential race
   without la migra asking stupid questions like,
      "Where're you coming from, boy?"
          What, did you not see me pull up just now?

Yeah, the Mexicans are definitely moving to Mars
Just as soon as they learn
how to breath in the pinche Martian air!

Mexi-Scam

When you buy enchiladas from a can
When you call Taco Bell real Mexican food
When you refuse to believe in Pancho Clos
When you disrespect your abuleos
When you sell drugs to your primos
When you refer to your family as wetbacks
When you steal from your brown neighbors
When you refuse to toil the dirt to produce food for a living
When you hunt for multiple partners just to get pregnant for a check
When you leave your pregnant girlfriend to impregnate another
When Uncle Sam is paying your child support bill for you
When you abandon your children for a good time
When your parents are raising your children
When a bronze goddess goes blonde to escape her heritage
When a beaner refuses to speak Spanish
When you call yourself High-Spanic
When you say you are bored with life unless you are getting high or drunk
When you refuse to learn about your ancestors
When you deny your Indianism
When you deny your Mexicanism
When you prefer to assimilate yourself to a bland-nothing America

When you are in perpetual denial of your brown self

-Yes. You!

You are scamming yourself and those around you!

The Cure

Suspend me for writing muscular words
While under the influence of metaphorical steroids
Words that deliver strong pain and pleasure
Words that seem more than they appear
Arrest me with your censorship
Ban my words, burn my books
Fill my biography with controversy
Deflate my grand ego with malicious, pure English
The cure you say that cures it all
That cures it all but what springs forth
From my unholy mouth, my demonized mind
Oblige yourself to cleanse me of my sin
With your cure that cures it all
That cures it all but me

The Trouble With Poets

The trouble with poets today
Is that they don't all write
About what troubles the minor majority
But what troubles the major minority

The trouble with that trouble
Is what keeps the poets today
From being branded formidable
Or well read, or well liked

Or un-mystified, or un-prejudice
Or well anthologized, or too scrutinized
Or our favorite, or poet laureates
In a sense that is, not in title

The trouble with poets today
Is that they all don't write about you
Growing up in some east coast metropolis
Or in some slim-lined, suburban home

Or a clean-cut, American pie metaphor
But a deranged division of its greater fraction
All of it from a different point of view
Most of it distinguishingly foreign to you

That is the trouble with poets today
That and the discombobulated, coffee house cup sizes

Then again, the trouble with poets today
Is that some don't write… about nothing at all

Casual Mexican

a Mexican

like a manly kind of pink
like listening to the quietness of a blaring radio
like the emptiness of a crowded mall
like the peace of a roaring war
or the stillness of a raging hurricane

you and I and them
casual Mexicans

like a slice of rotting pizza
like a hole in the ozone layer
like a one-dollar lottery win
like electricity in the water
or the heat of a free Sun

you and I and them
casual Mexicans

When Mexicans Attack!

For that whole border fence thing that's going on

I ain't the bad
that Hollywood makes me up to be

Yet, I am bad
        in a mad, Pancho Villa kind of way
        in a I'm-going-to-kick-your-ass kind of way
        in a rabies-infested-hatred-for-la-migra kind of way
        in a I-just-ate-three-jars-of-jalapeños-and-I-can't-find-
        the-bathroom kind of way

Ha! Ha! Just kidding
Yet, you really believe that
because Hollywood brain washed you
into believing that I really, really want to hurt you…

Huh?

The way things are going right now
maybe I'll start believing it myself

Latter Day Mexican Americans

Our lady Mary of the Connect the Dots
Down at the Church of the Latter Day Mexican Americans
Asked me if I wanted to place an order for tamales
To help fund the spaceship they were going to buy

To visit God
What?
To see if he was really faired skin with blue eyes
Or if he was brown and poor like the rest of us

To ask him if Hell was mainly for brown Indians
From the country formerly known as Aztlán
Or was it just a haven for country singers named Willie or Hank
Or maybe to ask how much more Anglo we must pretend to be

To at least smell the lemon pies made in Heaven's kitchen
I was going to say:
No, Sister Mary
I don't want to buy any damn tamales.

Besides, that clunker of a ship
That your preacher is looking into
Won't fly past Uranus.
Then I got to thinking that I would really like to know

If they make lemon pies in heaven

So I quickly responded:
How much is a dozen?

Sweet Jesus

Sweet Jesus!
La Migra stopped me
Asked me for some papers
With a sly, American smile
I produced a one-finger document
Needless to say
They thought my presentation was a little weak
Adding that it needed some revision
So I produced a second document
With my other hand
They were equally unimpressed
So after a few hours of interviews
Several musical chair dances around my car
They finally figured out
How American I really was
Despite my Mexican ancestry
Yet it does beg me to question:
Does my blatant arrogance bother them
As much as the color of my skin
Why do you question my allegiance
To this mighty, human race
What is it about me
About this glorious place
This United States Of Aztlán
Why must we bicker about ownership
In a world equally ours
God is surely shaking his head wondering:

Can't they all just get along
Sweet Jesus!

At The Border Of Ignorance

Lost between two worlds of translation
Between worlds of political disorder
Between worlds of bubbling borders
Happy for red turbulent ignorance

Rotting with sweet dark contempt
Feeling the rightful wrongness
Yet unable to describe it all
Lost between the eloquent "Mexican-Me"

And suspicious of the coconut sellout
Wondering who is actually conducting this sale
Reeling only on the inner soul
To decide what is good for it

What is not
We, cosmic ones, are here
At the edge of the Mexican-American dream
Blocked by global arrogance

At the rim of pandemic ignorance
THEY will surely come to you
To your edge, your border
To kill

Your dream
Your soul

Your wrongness
Your contempt

Your ignorance
So fellow brown humans
Be not ignorant of THEY
For THEY are watching you too, cabrón!

The Plight

I invite you into my soul
Somewhere underneath my dark skin
Where small differences divide us
Like large oceans on opposite coasts

I invite you into my soul
Somewhere behind my dark, brown eyes
Where deep dialects are clichés emphasized
By xenophobic demons in Hollywood

I invite you into my soul
Somewhere between Tejas y Mejico
Where death bleaches great dreams
Of otherwise hard-working people

I invite you into my soul
Just once
For a little stroll

Are You Tired of US Yet?

Are you tired
of drinking cervesas at the local cantina
of eating delicious tacos and enchiladas
of having many reasons to throw a fiesta

Are you tired
of your home or office getting cleaned
of your lawn looking nice and pretty
of your fancy old cars running again

Are you tired
of getting elected to political office
of having culture and spice added to the American melting pot
of having a scapegoat for your immigration problems

It's no wonder that you are tired of US
everything has practically been done for you
      …maybe you should try doing it for your self

What Does It Matter

I am violent as I am beautiful
I am damned as I am blessed
I am happy as I am unhappy
I am love as I am hate
I am free as I am slave
I am red, white, and green
As I am red, white, and blue
I am you don't you see
As you should see that you are me
I am running in the street
As I am lying dead in it
I am el Rio Bravo Del Norte
As I am el Rio Grande
I am the Aztec-descendant attacking the walls of the Alamo
As I am the Aztec-descendant defending it from inside
I am me because I am you
I am straight as I am crooked
I am brown as I am white
I am red as I am black
I am yellow as I am any other color
I am you as you are me
I am nothing as I am everything
I am human as I appear inhuman
I am human like you are human
I am substance because you are substance
Whatever you have decided we should be
Matters not when I still love you

All of you living on this planet
And those that have already left it

Shallow Water

Face down under shallow water I will lay
that will be your final judgment on me

You will never see me fight like the underdog that I am
you will never hear me speak the language you call your own
you will never taste the culture I bring with me
you will never love the things that make me different

Instead you will make me see ignorance
you will make me hear hate
you will make me taste my blood
you will make me love death over pain

You will pass judgment on me
through a high-powered rifle scope
as I will lay face down
in the shallow water of the Rio Grande

With my eyes willingly open
with my ears unobstructed
with my tongue ready for the taste
with my heart gasping for fleeting oxygenated cells

To catch that last glimpse of hope
streaming by like the last of my soul
floating south with the river
with that American dream

that you have made impossible for me
that I will never see, hear, taste or love

Antebellum Again

To be brown like me
Is like being free
Only in a metaphorical society
Is like bean and cheese
Instead of bread and butter
Is like practicing freedom
Under watchful nativist's fences
As much as I may love you
It is not like you
Under pretty, fair skin
Behind blue-sky eyes
Where the struggle of western expansion
Is a celebration of your character
Instead of the truthful devastation
Of the cultures that already existed
I can't remove the tan of my skin
As easily as you removed us from our land
However, if you insist
On this dark path of removal
The only domain I will let you conquer
Is the heated one below

Gunfighters At Bland Canyon

Speaking of course in my best southern drawl
Somewhere in a place called Oblivion, I say
A Mexican is always ready for a gunfight
Yet, I didn't bring my pistolas
I came willingly strapped with two nuclear bombs
Full of strong, bronze Chicano poems
My intention is to blow this Bland Canyon
Between the deep confines of your mind
Radiate what ethnic insecurities you harbor
Into feel good, tequila blues
Shift the ensuing nuclear winter fallout
Into one huge festive, poetic Cinco de Mayo
Then let you die peacefully punch drunk
On wicked margarita messages of love
Gunfighter, I am your messiah of finality
Where what you once knew ends forever
Where your mind steps in line with your treason
Where you are eye to eye to woman-less nipples
Where you are now without words and I
Swiftly fire away those perpetual ancient incantations
That spoke against conquests of many nations
Way before your ancestors knew what existed
Beyond those beautiful, blue Atlantic waters

Stereotypical: A Zombie Poem... Or Is It?

Trying not to be, but I can't help it
You can pretty much tell who is or not
I mean, who moans about work constantly?
Who is always trying to get so close?
Who is always struggling to walk or talk?
Who is always late to our group meetings?

I tell you, I know one when I see one
So if I see something, I'll do something
That something on this list is Ricardo
He is a zombie if ever there was
I mean, look at him. He dresses funny.
He smells horrible. He says my name weird.

I just know I'm right! So who is with me?
Let's vote to see who will bash his brains in

What To Expect When You're Suspecting

Beavers are adorable creatures
With that I have no argument
But let's not talk about yours
Because there's no blessing there

Guilty is my cholo mind
That suspects what's in the store
Where empty minds and empty souls
Are walking around like zombies

I suspect that you are expecting
That my mouth remains in silence
I won't sit so idly by
While you try to rob my culture

Nah, I ain't threatening to take over
Just saying that I'm watching
So you don't impregnate the world
With vacant words and raw stupidity

Lengua-Legal*

They want us to stop speaking in this tongue
Like we came from another planet
Like strangers in a stranger's land
Imagining the aliens living among us
They want us to stop speaking Spanish
Because, they say, it is not what we speak in America
It is in fact un-American to speak other than in English
Because this Spanish language comes from another country
I do not know who your English teacher was
My nativist, nationalist, English-only American
But English came from England, not America
And we all have immigrant ancestry according to your own books
Not just the Mexicans, who are only immigrants
By the virtue of a treaty created for your own benefit, pilgrim

*said in Spanish of course

Those Doors

Outside
Outside that wooden door
Is another door
That opens up to yet another door
Beyond that door who knows
Perhaps another door
That leads outside of this reality
Away from unclear minds
Where brown is a color
That traps a soul to choices
Outside those doors
That remain shut
Not because they are
But because we let them
Why do we let them?
Because they are red, white, yellow, and black

I'm going to take a vicious chainsaw
To those multicolored doors
Screaming for multicultural mercy
To find my way out that door
Just outside my reality
Just outside my mind
Just outside my door

I See Brown People

I see brown people
When I sit to eat a salad
The onions
The tomatoes
The lettuce

I see brown people
When I touch the walls of a new home
The floors
The cabinets
The plumbing

I see brown people
When I stop to rest the night at a hotel
The bed
The carpet
The toilet

I see brown people
When I see rich people
Their cars
Their homes
Their children

I see brown people
In long unemployment lines
Long commodity lines

Long prison roll calls
Long funeral processions

I see brown people everywhere
Yet, where are they
In history books?
In schools?
In the world?

Color

Like that upon our living flesh
That at unexpected times determines
How some of us treat our others
Humans of different pigments of color

Some a darker shade of evil
From destruction and discrimination
Others more so that of the clouds
Holding to inner self-determination

Funny is the thing how a tint
Clearly dictates to you, to me
Where our innards are interchangeable
Unaffected by any dye that you can see

After a century you would figure
That color was just an antique word
That it didn't describe race or culture
Economic status or who dies by your sword

Yet, that is the peculiar meaning
Of so appealing a human stain
Color, as in nature, forever lasting
As is the wars man carries in its name

What If It Happened In America?

Arizona's SB 1040

Whatever happened to
Truth, justice, and the American way
Whatever happened to
America, land of the free, the proud
Whatever happened to
Good neighbors, apple pie, and comic books
Whatever happened to
America, the great, grand melting pot
Whatever happened to
America, the beautiful, land of immigrants
A year or two down the road
From this dehumanizing law
The last of the immigrants in heavy, kryptonite chains
Arrested, deported, demoralized
The greatest of ourselves
Kal-El, the last son of Krypton

For The Mother Of My Half-Mexican Children

You sure aren't a Mexican
Yet here you are, marching at my side
Shouting "¡Que Viva!" while holding up red, UFW flags
Celebrating César Chávez's ideas for a better, Mexican-American future

You sure aren't a Mexican
Yet how you dared to marry me and have my children
Despite your discriminating family's intentions
After I first showed up at your shot-gun, dinner table

You sure aren't a Mexican
Yet you can roll tortillas with the best of them
Yet your menudo is so delicious, you have to lie
Telling my overly-satisfied relatives that I made it instead

You sure aren't a Mexican
But maybe you are, somewhere under your delicate, fair skin

If I Was White I Would Write…

or another reason to hate Chicano poets

Poems about my clear, blue eyes
about my clean, fair complexion
about my pretty, blonde hair
Poems about my augmented, trophy wife
about my obedient, 2.5 children
about my multi-dollar corporate job
Poems about my shiny, picket, white fence
about my nicely painted, two-story home
about my brand-new, fancy car
Poems about expensive vacations to somewhere exotic
about how much minorities piss you off
when they complain about the things they don't have

Well, you won't get those verses from me
Since I can't write… because I ain't white

El Corrido De El Librotraficante

En el estado de la Arizona
Esta una gobernadora muy bocona
Pasando siempre la mala palabra
Encontra mi gente, linda mejicana

Con eso comenzo todo este guato
De remover lo nuestro con contrato
Por las escuelas entre los cuartos
Libros escribidos por nuestros vatos

Ponte trucha, chicas y chicanos
De aqui semos y no los vamos
Nuestra palabra es nuestra historia
Da le madre hasta la victoria

Entre Tejas por todos lados
Comenzaron los librostraficanos
Para Nuevo Mejico de paraditas
A tomar tequila con compadristas

Despues llegaron a la Arizona
Para darle lumbre a la comenzona
Porque aqui se acaba, les dice Diaz
Y porque este jale ya no valia

De mente a frente fueron cambiando
Estos gueys menos confiando

Hasta por fin ya se calmaron
Y los chicanos con fe ganaron

Pues, si te dicen que estas en mal
Por tu color de cuero o lengua tal
Cantales los echos del caravan
De librotraficantes y ya veran

Prayer Sayer

Padre nuestro que estás en los cielos
Santificado sea tu Nombre
Venga tu reino
Hágase tu voluntad
En la tierra como en el cielo
Danos hoy el pan de este día
y perdona nuestras deudas
como nosotros perdonamos nuestros deudores
y no nos dejes caer en al tentación
sino que líbranos del malo.

Asi sea

Amen

Say a prayer today
Say a prayer today for that young man
at the gun shop thinking of shooting up
his high school tomorrow

Say a prayer today
Say a prayer today for that forty-year old
dreaming of fulfilling a horrific fantasy
with an unsuspecting teenager

Say a prayer today
Say a prayer today for that young father

celebrating way too much with friends at the local bar
now in his car about to drive away

Say a prayer today
Say a prayer today for the leaders of countries
who spend too much time tweeting about war
instead of talking to people face to face about peace

Say a prayer today
Say a prayer today because tomorrow is not guaranteed
Because we are not perfect and only our creator
whatever name you choose to use
can help us and stop us when we have gone too far

Say a prayer today
Say a prayer today instead of mourning tomorrow
asking God "why" when we didn't even try
Believe that with prayer we can stop tragedy
so when we see something, say it to God as well

God help us!
Say a prayer today
Say a prayer today
Say a prayer today

Our Father who art in heaven,
hallowed be thy name.
Thy kingdom come.
Thy will be done
on earth as it is in heaven.

Give us this day our daily bread,
and forgive us our trespasses,
as we forgive those who trespass against us,
and lead us not into temptation,
but deliver us from evil.
For thine is the kingdom,
and the power,
and the glory,
for ever and ever.

Amen.

English As A Second Language (ESL) Civics Lesson I: A Slice Of "The Declaration Of Independence"

(a)

We hold (Like a cute, newborn baby; not these ugly, three-toad, monkey-tail ones.) ***these truths*** (More like lies, depending on how many billions you stand to make from it and how much of a black-snake, pipeline you can shove up the American masses.) ***to be self-evident*** (Equivalent to "fake-news" where it is obvious that only those people in power can tell the only truth.), ***that all men*** (Clarification: only rich, old, white men who hide their immigrant background really well and not those other "bad hombres" or "nasty women" nor any of those other liberal

(b)

"Lifesaver" flavors.) ***are created equal*** (Exchange rate not measured by American standards. Maybe by some third-world country values like England, Canada, and most especially, damned Mexico!),

that they are endowed (By the way, most powerful rich, white men have an average six-inch penis according to a recent report by Forbes Magazine among Fortune 500 business leaders and their "peters.") ***by their Creator*** (Oh yeah, remember HIM? The same GOD who is now banned from American public schools, sports events, and public arenas where HE is

(c)

most certainly needed!) ***with certain unalienabl***e (please don't mistake this for Mexican citizens or Martian people. They are still alienable… very alienable.) ***Rights*** (don't worry about this word because you don't have any… unless your daddy is super rich! This is an antiquated word used to make you feel better.), ***that among these are Life*** (Don't worry about it. You don't have one.), ***Liberty*** (That would be that French gal in the harbor… not the "freedoms" you think you get.) **and the pursuit** (Like when the cops or immigration are chasing you down. You know

(d)

the drill.) ***of Happiness*** (Now that is damned funny! That does not exist unless you can buy it the good, old fashioned way: Filthy Money and some Good Ol' Oppression.).---

Holy Sonnet No. 1

Jesus Saves! Jesus Saves!
But does he care for the color of your skin
Or if you wear pants or skirts
Does he care where you bank
Or which church you thinks is right

Jesus Saves! Jesus Saves!
But does he care if you are young or old
Does it matter where you went to school
Does he care for which team you pray
Does he think much about where you live

Jesus Saves! Jesus Saves!
Reads the side of the landscaper's van
Savings Lawns One At A Time!
¡Se Habla Español!

I Am Chupacabra

I am chupacabra, hear me growl
Through the decades of infamy
Through the media of lies, dark of deception
Through the conversation of who or what is real
Where the media is in fact its own myth

I am chupacabra, hear me growl
At the insanity of death blamed on me
At the ghosts of witnesses pointing their finger the other way
Where rouge restaurants and coyotes are to blame
For a painted, bloody landscaped framed around me

I am chupacabra, hear me growl
At classical mythology and urban myths
Whose proposal of me is non-existential
Whose proponents deny a rightful throne
To me, my one and only true character

I am chupacabra, hear me growl
With the anger of pre-Columbian culture
That perpetuates its mystical figures, their Lloronas
Their mixed, non-conflicting, Christian-paganism
Their bronze-colored Virgin De Guadalupe

I am chupacabra, hear me growl
For it may be the last time in your history
For it threatens to kick me out of the already sick gate

Where many other creatures are denied immigration
Into the land of that great, sweet promise of imagination

I am chupacabra, hear me growl

Jalapeño Propagandist

For Trinidad Sanchez, Jr. (1943-2006)

If you are going to live in this America
You must eat a lot of jalapeños
Jalapeños, like Mexicans, are everywhere
And America is a jalapeño genius
An America without it
Is an America without spice, without flavor
There must not be an American
That has not endured the Mean Green
It is a true rite of American passage
For all those born and born to be
And any others getting here to be free
It is unconstitutional not to try
To eat them, laugh or cry

This was Jose, the Jalapeño Juicy Juice
Bringing you all this Jalapeño Jazz
Brought to you by our sponsor
The Council of Jalapeños for America
Because sooner or later
Everyone needs a Mexican…
I mean a jalapeño, in their life

What Can Brown Do For You?

I was thinking that perhaps
it could get you drunk
thrown in jail
out of bars
mistaken for another
accused of stealing
or at least eyeballing something to take
treated like a foreigner
even though you were born right here in America

Then I thought that maybe
it could remind people
of YOUR mighty ancestry
the greatness of the Aztecs
the Mayas, the Toltec
the grand totality of Central America
the contributions to math and science
to architecture and religion
to poetry and mythology

Then I further contemplated that
brown is sexy, exotic
in case you didn't notice
a natural aphrodisiac
works well on the fairer skins
it could ultimately get you laid
more times than you could count to a hundred in Spanish

Yeah baby, that's what brown can do for you!

Dr. Jesus' Presents: It's "Kiss A Mexican" Everyday

Hey, hey, hey, hurray
It's "Kiss A Mexican" everyday
Don't you diss. Don't you hiss
Don't you dare miss with that kiss

We'll wash your clothes
We'll plow your fields
We'll pick your food
And make your meals

Hey, hey, hey, hurray
It's "Kiss A Mexican" everyday
Don't you diss. Don't you hiss
Don't you dare miss with that kiss

We'll wash your pets
We'll pick your trash
We'll sing you songs
To earn your cash

Hey, hey, hey, hurray
It's "Kiss A Mexican" everyday
Don't you diss. Don't you hiss
Don't you dare miss with that kiss

We'll fix your homes
We'll fix your trucks

We'll fix your problems
Yeah that's us

Hey, hey, hey, hurray
It's "Kiss A Mexican" everyday
Don't you diss. Don't you hiss
Don't you dare miss with that kiss

Make Tortillas Not War

My fellow Americans
Make tortillas not war!
Make tortillas not war!

Let us get fat with peace
Not gluttonous with hate
Let us clog our arteries
With the great things in life
Not occlude our taxed veins
With stray bullets and strife

Dear fellow Americans
Make tortillas not war!
Make tortillas not war!

Let us clean our bean bowls
Instead of blood from the floor
Let us smell our beautiful cultures
Not impose it on others
Let us sit at full tables
Instead of full funerals

My multi-colored Americans
I say to you
Make tortillas not war!
Make tortillas not war!

Life Around The Tortilla Curtain

Does Mexican cheese
come from Mexican cows?
Do they wade into the Rio Grande
and if so, are they illegal too?

They say they want to put up a fence
all along the Rio Grande
That's great vato!
It will help the cows stay in one place
To help separate the brown cows
from the white cows
it will help in the mix up
of Mexican cheese and American cheese
just like in the supermercado
keep you from messing up your enchiladas

By the way, that will also help separate
regular white milk from chocolate milk
I love chocolate milk
but I can only have so much
it's too rich you know
so I have to regularly drink
regular white milk

It goes with everything I guess

That's great that they want to put up a fence

to.. como se dice? A si
accentuate the difference between
Mexican cheese and American cheese
chocolate milk and regular white milk

The North American continent
what a great place for diarrhea
...I mean dairy products
sorry, mi ingles not so good

Don't Drop The Taco

Whatever you do, don't drop the taco
Because the Mexicans are watching you
And they don't take too kindly to your blind
Disrespect for their food or their culture

Whatever you do, don't drop the taco
Even if you're questioned by the police
And you know they are about to make you
Get down to the ground, make love to the dirt

Whatever you do, don't drop the taco
Even when you're tagging that stupid wall
Writing how Trump can suck your you know what
While you're getting high on those spray can fumes

Whatever you do, don't drop the taco
Even when stopped at border checkpoint
One hand on the wheel, other on the prize
Wanting to show them that they're number one

Whatever you do, don't drop the taco
Even if your girl wants to hold your hand
But you can't even hold up your own pants
With family packs of tacos in each arm

So always remember, no matter what
Whether the devil is after your butt

Or you're making love to your step-sister
Whatever you do, don't drop the taco

Tell Me What?

Did I tell you? So, I didn't tell you.
That Mejico is never going to
Pay for that racist, xenophobic wall
In no kind of way nor in cold, green cash

Did I tell you? So, I didn't tell you.
That lush, healthy fields don't harvest themselves
Who's going to pay better wages to
Those who don't want field jobs in the first place

Did I tell you? So, I didn't tell you.
That these kooky ideas by rich men
Are simply that and only spread fear to
Other rich men who can't see blue from sky

Did I tell you? So, I didn't tell you.
Most things bothering you are just made up

A Promising Letter To A Worrisome Trump

If you were worried about Mexicans
There is no real honest need to do so.
Do what you will. Say what you want to.
No need to worry. We'll get over it!

You are the president. You are in charge.
You do what you must for all the people
Especially those who voted you in.
No need to worry. We'll get over it!

Sign your executive orders, your laws
Your special arrangements with companies.
Break what rules you need to bring about change!
No need to worry. We'll get over it!

And go ahead and build your mighty great wall.
No need to worry. We'll get over it!

Bad Hombre

I.

He says proudly in a bad, Spanish drawl
Like in those old, western, cowboy movies
That my father loved when he was alive
Where those white heroes in their big, white hats
Killed all the mean, bad guys and saved the day
Where happy endings weren't really happy
Not for the indigenous on both sides
Of another unpopular topic
Which brings up the point easy to forget
"Mexicans" is a common name for "us"
The descendants of First Nation people
"English," like "Spanish," is a foreign tongue
Fairly new here by history's measure
So, what's so evil about us, again?

II.

Maybe he's dreaming of cowboy westerns
That clean-cut sheriff out to clear the town
Except he's not a working vaquero
Nor has he ever played one on TV
Shooting off six-gun bullet words of hate
Like so many with mastery of speech
"Mexican Grease," when my father was young
"Get-back Wetback," when I was growing up

Now in the age of my grandson's young life
The Mexican callout is "Bad Hombre"
Romanticized in one moment of time
A put-down, get them out of town, today
Feeding prejudicial fear and distaste
Go home, bad gringo with your mad lingo

Humpity Trumpity

Humpity Trumpity will fall from his wall
The same one he'll build against one and all
A wall deep and long, so crooked and tall
To keep all the Mexicans from coming to call
To stir up more issues that hate and enthrall
You think that he cares, that mouthy meatball?

Humpity Trumpity will fall from his wall
He won't be worth saving, no, not all
Most definitely be his biggest shortfall
No super supremacists, no Neanderthals
No Richie Rich friends, or kooky oddballs
Will do much to fix him, none therewithal

Humpity Trumpity will fall from his wall
That's what he builds and he'll build very tall
To Mexicans he'll beg, he'll barter, he'll call
To come and to help him from his great, grand fall
Those rapists, those murderers, if you can recall
Is what he once called them and did appall

Humpity Trumpity will fall from his wall
A symbol of fear, a xenophobic pitfall
Clogging great hope like cholesterol
Brown people dig holes, under it crawl
So build the wall high, beyond the eyeball
As thick as you want, sun-up to night-fall

Yes, Humpity Trumpity will fall from his wall
Many who cared, will not care at all
Speeding downhill, a dirty snowball
For justice will come from God's Protocol
Those who do evil bring on their downfall
No matter their station, how big or how small

Screw The Wall!

Screw the wall! Kill all the Mexicans!
Screw the wall! Kill all the Mexicans!

Leave no barrier between real thieves, the rich
Their exploitation of the poor, the indigenous
Leave no barrier between the spoiled; their roots
Fanatical Christianity; mixed unions conflicting you
Leave no barrier between your perfect language; theirs
A 2nd class citizenship; a quiet, peace-less genocide
Leave no barrier between yourself; the uncertain "them"
Your pompous, clean skin; their beat down, brown rinds

Screw the wall! Kill all the Mexicans!
Screw the wall! Kill all the Mexicans!

Leave no mystery between your tax dollars; your waste
Of who is left unconquered; of who will toil your land
Leave no mystery between who cleans you; your soiled homes
Pampering your wild children; placing flavor into your meals
Leave no mystery between "those" in unemployment lines
Who take all your "good" jobs; your riddled, American pie
Leave no mystery between your scapegoats; your personal agendas
Things you hate; things you want to get rid of anyways

Screw the wall! Kill all the Mexicans!
Screw the wall! Kill all the Mexicans!

Besides heaven is a much better place for the Mexicans
Where beautiful, great, gringo angels now tend to them
Besides heaven is a much better place for the Mexicans
Where the brown poor don't worry about the sickly rich
Besides heaven is a much better place for the Mexicans
Where the self-imposed important are important no more
Besides heaven is a much better place for the Mexicans
Where rich utopias are no longer carried on broken, brown backs

Screw a Mexican! Kill all the walls!
Screw a Mexican! Kill all the walls!

Screw The White Man!

Screw Whitey! Screw Whitey!

Don't you hate it when they walk around
All uptight with that political correctness crap
Always trying to conform, themselves first
To rules you know that they know are awkward
Then begging the rest of us in America to join in
Yet we're having too much fun pointing the truth out

Screw Whitey! Screw Whitey!

Don't you hate it when they walk around
Always apologizing for things they didn't do
Things their forefathers did a long time ago
Things their grandfathers used to do but no more
So they try to buy it all out with green American cash
I mean sure the money is good, but good grief!

Screw Whitey! Screw Whitey!

Don't you hate it when they walk around
All depressed because they think they're in charge
That God made them boss over all other pigments
Always acting like a great breasted woman
Trying to make us nurse from her huge, ample tits
To eat from her helping of White-American pie

Screw Whitey! Screw Whitey!

Don't' you hate it when they walk around
In desperate attempts to make US a better people
With fresh clean thoughts that are mostly weird to us
Saying "Please Listen To Us Because We Know Better"
Knowing it takes a much stronger slap across the face
To make us pay attention to their plain proposal of life

Screw Whitey! Screw Whitey!

Don't you hate it when they walk around
Devoid of a natural, rightful, wholesome life
Sadly, not enough of them getting their required fornication
I mean in a hard, in and out, good old fashion kind of way
They need love from whatever ethnicity is willing to give it
Make this Great Melting Pot sizzle with some good spicing

Screw Whitey! Screw Whitey!

Yeah, you know they need a good screwing
Now everybody turn to the nearest white person
Give them a great big hug. Tell them you love them
Tell them it's gonna be okay but they need to cut their shit out
Tell them you got their back... or front... or whatever.
But this is all they are getting tonight... maybe... if their cool with that

Screw Whitey! Screw Whitey!

ACKNOWLEDGEMENTS

A Promising Letter To A Worrisome Trump first appeared in *FEIPOL: Festival Internacional De Poesia Latinoamericana Anthology,* 2018.

Antebellum Again first appeared in *SA Arts United Magazine,* 2012.

Are You Tired Of Us Yet? for appeared in *Poets And Dreamers,* 2018.

At The Border Of Ignorance first appeared in *Writers Of The Rio Grande Website,* 2011.

Bad Hombre first appeared in *Winward Review,* 2017.

Casual Mexican first appeared in *The Muse,* 2006.

Chupacabra Lives Matter first appeared in *2:00 AM: A Poetry Group,* 2020.

Color first appeared in *The Dreamcatcher: Awaken The Sleeping Poet Festival Anthology,* Laurel Crown Foundation, 2009.

Don't Drop The Taco first appeared in Radius: From *The Center To The Edge,* 2017.

El Corrido De El Librotraficante first appeared in *La Bloga,* 2012.

For The Mother Of My Half-Mexican Children first appeared in *The Journal Of Latina Critical Feminism, 3rd Edition*, 2019.

Free first appeared in *di-verse-city: The Austin International Poetry Festival Anthology*, 2010.

Gunfighters At Bland Canyon first appeared in *Voices Along The River: The 12th Annual Edition Of The San Antonio Poetry Fair*, 2009.

Humpity Trumpity first appeared in *Ain't Gonna Be Treated This Way: Celebrating Woody Guthrie, Poems Of Protest And Resistance*, 2017.

I Am Chupacabra first appeared in *Boundless: The Anthology Of The Rio Grande Valley International Poetry Festival*, 2012.

I Am Juan In The Fields first appeared in *The Enigmatists*, 2011.

I See Brown People first appeared in *di-verse-city: The Austin International Poetry Festival Anthology*, 2009.

It's Not Easy Being Greasy first appeared in *Elegant Rage: A Poetic Tribute To Woody Guthrie, Village Books Press*, 2012.

Jalapeño Propagandist first appeared in *Langdon Review Of The Arts In Texas*, 2011.

Latter Day Mexican Americans first appeared in *Voices De La*

Luna, 2009.

Life Around The Tortilla Curtain first appeared in *Live! From La Pryor: The Poetry of Juan Manuel Perez: A Zavala Country Native Son, Volume 1, 2014.*

Make Tortillas Not War first appeared in *Voices De La Luna, 2008.*

Mexicans Appear Violent first appeared in *Writers Of The Rio Grande Website, 2011.*

Mexicans On The Move Again first appeared in *WUI: Written Under the Influence of Trinidad Sanchez, Jr., 2011.*

Mexi-Scam first appeared in *The Packing House Review, 2019.*

Prayer Sayer first appeared in *FEIPOL: Festival Internacional De Poesia Latinoamericana Anthology,, 2018.*

Push Farther My Father Said first appeared in *New Texas: A Journal Of Literature And Culture, 2012.*

Shallow Water first appeared in *O' Dark Heaven: A Response to Suzette Haden Elgin's Definition of Horror, 2009.*

Sweet Jesus first appeared in *Boundless: The Anthology Of The Rio Grande Valley International Poetry Festival, 2011.*

Tell Me What? first appeared in *Radius: From The Center To The Edge, 2017.*

The Cat From The Other Side Of The Tracks first appeared in *The Beatest State In the Union: An Anthology Of Beat Texas Writings, 2016.*

The Cure first appeared in *Concho River Review, 2011.*

The Onion Picker's Dream first appeared in *Writers Of The Rio Grande Website, 2011.*

The Plight first appeared in *Writers Of The Rio Grande Website, 2011.*

The Trouble With Poets first appeared in *descant: Fort Worth's Journal Of Fiction and Poetry, 2012.*

Those Doors first appeared in *Inkwell Echoes, 2008-2009: The Anthology Of The San Antonio Poets Association, 2009.*

Today We March first appeared in *2:00 AM: A Poetry Group, 2019.*

What Can Brown Do For You first appeared in *Boundless: The Anthology Of The Rio Grande Valley International Poetry Festival, 2009.*

What Does It Matter first appeared in *Gifts Of The Great Spirit: White Buffalo Contest Anthology, 2012.*

What If it Happened In America? first appeared in *Elegant Rage: A Poetic Tribute To Woody Guthrie, 2012.*

What To Expect When You're Suspecting first appeared in *Writers Of The Rio Grande Website, 2011.*

When Mexicans Attack! first appeared in *WUI: Written Under the Influence of Trinidad Sanchez, Jr., 2011.*

Juan Manuel Pérez, a Mexican-American poet of indigenous descent and the current Poet Laureate for Corpus Christi, Texas (2019-2020), is the author of Another Menudo Sunday (2007), O' Dark Heaven: A Response to Suzette Haden Elgin's Definition of Horror (2009), WUI: Written Under the Influence of Trinidad Sanchez, Jr. (2011), Live From La Pryor: The Poetry of Juan Manuel Perez: A Zavala Country Native Son, Volume 1 (2014), and Sex, Lies, and Chupacabras (2015), as well as, the co-editor of The Call Of The Chupacabra (2018). He is the 2011-2012 San Antonio Poets Association Poet Laureate and the Lone Star State's only EL Chupacabras Poet Laureate (For Life). The former Gourd Dancer for the Memphis Tia Piah Big River Clan Warrior Society is also a Pushcart Prize Nominee as well as a SEATTAH Scholar (Striving For Excellence And Accountability In The Teaching Of Traditional American History) through the University Of Dallas. Juan is a ten-year Navy Corpsman/Combat Marine Medic with experience in the 1991 Persian Gulf War with the 2nd Marines and the 1992 Hurricane Andrew Relief Marine Air Group Task Force. This two-time Teacher of the Year, along with his wife, Malia (a three-time Teacher of the Year), is a co-founder of The House of the Fighting Chupacabras Press. Currently, Juan worships his Creator, teaches public high school history, writes poetry, and chases chupacabras in the Texas Coastal Bend Area.